Screenplay Format
Made (Stupidly) Easy

Vol.4 of the ScriptBully
Screenwriting Collection

by Michael Rogan
Editor, ScriptBully Magazine

Published in USA by: ScriptBully Magazine

Michael Rogan

© Copyright 2018

ISBN-13: 978-1-970119-03-9
ISBN-10: 1-970119-03-9

Table of Contents

About the Author

Michael Rogan is a former Hollywood screenplay reader, optioned screenwriter and editor of ScriptBully magazine - an inbox periodical devoted to helping screenwriters write well...and get paid.

He is also the owner of the world's most neurotic Jack Russell Terrier.

And has made it his mission in life to rid the world of movies about trucks that turn into robots.

A Special FREE Gift for You!

If you'd like FREE instant access to my seminar "7 Secrets to a Kick-Ass and Marketable Screenplay" then head over to **ScriptBully.com/Free**. (What else you gonna do? Watch another "Twilight" movie?!)

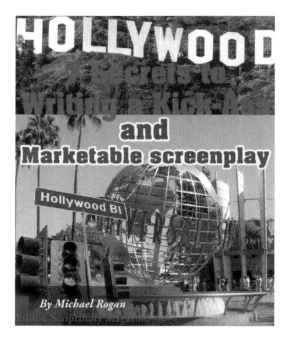

A Super Quick Note About the Formatting of This Book

Don't know whether you've ever tried formatting text for a print book.

Under normal circumstances — such as a cheesy novel about pale, teenage vampires — it can be challenging.

But trying to display the many tab/spacing issues that come up with screenplay format can be harder than finding an action movie that DOESN'T star Nicolas Cage.

I've done my very best to preserve correct formatting, as best I can, in this book.

But in some cases that was nearly impossible.

So, as not to totally confuse you with the weird formatting, I'd like to also offer you a couple of FREE BONUSES as a thank you for buying my book. (And to make sure you get the best screenplay format info I can provide!)

Here's what you get:

FREE PDF version of this book. (Just drop me a line at Michael@scriptbully.com with the subject line "Gimme My Format PDF" and I'll send it right over.) This should help keep things clear and give you a reference as you read this book.

A sample screenwriting scene that uses all of the techniques outlined in this book can be found at my blog: http://scriptbully.com/screenplay-format-sample

Okay…enough of my jabbering. On with the show!

Prologue: "We Find the Defendants Incredibly Guilty"

"Great ability develops and reveals itself increasingly with every new assignment."

-Baltasar Gracian

Screenplay format isn't rocket science. It doesn't require an advanced degree in Film Criticism or attendance at a $2,000 weekend screenwriting seminar in Maui.

And unlike more abstract parts of the craft of screenwriting, its standards are actually straightforward.

But hang out at any number of screenwriting forums and you'll see a good majority of the questions aren't about structure or characters or plot

sequences or writing better jokes or how to get
Megan Fox to return your calls.

It's questions like:

- How do I write a flashback?

- How do I introduce a character who has
  no name?

- How do I write a montage?

- How do I write an action scene?

- How do I write telephone calls?

- Is a car an interior or an exterior?

All of these questions hint at a single insecurity:
How do I write a script I plan to send to managers

and agents without looking like a total noob?

Worry not, young Jedi. That's what this book is all about.

But before we dig in, we need to do some housekeeping. Namely, answering a few questions upfront:

Question No.1: Why the #$%*# Do I Have to Learn Screenplay Format?

This reminds me of the old joke about drummers:

Question: How many drummers does it take to change a light bulb?
Answer: Don't they have a machine for that?

Point being: Why learn about script format, when there's a perfectly good $200 piece of software that'll take care of your formatting needs.

And, yes, it's true. Software such as Final Draft or Movie Magic will keep your margins intact and your spacing inbounds.

But software WON'T tell you how to set up a shot heading on a spaceship.

Or tell you how to boost the pacing in your action-movie car chase.

Or show you the right way to use parentheticals. (Answer: Sparingly, if at all.)

A lot of screenwriters think turning in a script in FDR (Final Draft) format is enough to show they belong in the business.

But one errant use of "WE PULL BACK TO SEE" or "THE CAMERA PULLS BACK TO REVEAL" can brand you as amateur quicker than a "Walker, Texas Ranger" DVD collection.

Good screenplay format isn't about following rules. It's about making things easier for the reader. (And don't you think the reader suffers enough, having to slog through endless "vampire/zombie romance" specs?)

So, as you learn the proper use of ANGLE ON and DISSOLVE and MOVING WITH, remember it's not about the number of dials on a Marshall half-stack amplifier.

It's about the music it makes.

Question No.2: Do I Need to Buy Screenwriting Software?

Yes. You do.

I highly recommend you buy one of the professional screenwriting tools out there, such as Final Draft (Amazon link: http://scriptbully.com/finaldraft) or Movie Magic (Amazon link: http://scriptbully.com/moviemagic). Solutions like this should set you back no more than 200 bucks or so.

And yes you COULD create a ghetto tricked-out word doc template to use. But the money you THINK you're saving will be lost in all THAT frickin' time you're spending on resizing margins.

But if you really want to do it the hard way, or are short on funds, here's a quick breakdown of how to set up your margins manually: http://www.simplyscripts.com/WR_format.html

Again, I don't recommend it. Your formatting can quickly get out of control. But it ll do in a pinch. (You know, before you sell your spec for $425,000.)

Question No.3: The Format You Recommend Looks Different Than Stuff I See in Published Screenplays...What Gives?

Well, this could be for a variety of reasons. One, you might look at a shooting script. Shooting scripts are designed to help the crew — namely the cinematographer and director of photography — from killing each other.

Shooting scripts are technical and filled with tons of camera-placement information no writer SHOULD ever presume to write. (Nothing causes a script to smell "amateur" like overly complicated camera directions.)

Another reason the screenplay you're reading looks different is its age. Read a few pages of the thoroughly entertaining "Butch Cassidy and The Sundance Kid" — by the Dean of Screenwriters, William Goldman — and you might think your script needs a bunch of "CUT TOs" and long expository paragraphs to show its screenwriting mettle.

But we live in a different age. (One where 140 characters is presumed to be enough to express a single, coherent thought.)

And keeping things short and lean is not only the modern style, but it's also the BEST way to express your story in a visual and powerful way.

Promise of This Book

I can't promise that nailing all the techniques in this book will get your script sold. But for the same reason you wear an overpriced, itchy suit to a job interview, or remove pictures of yourself downing tequila shots from your Facebook profile before you fill out a job application, proper screenplay format makes you look like a professional.

It makes you look dedicated.

It makes you look like you know what the hell you're doing.

And, believe me, there are many writers out there who don't know what the hell they're doing, you'll be noticed for following the guidelines I'm about to show you.

And getting noticed can change your life.

Chapter 1:
Location, Location, Location

"Simple's the most sophisticated thing of all."

-Ina Garten

Shot headings, otherwise known as scene headings or sluglines, form the backbone of screenplay format. And like my favorite band of all time, "The Violent Femmes," they are highly underrated.

There are two basic forms of shot headings:

- Master Shot Headings
- Secondary Shot Headings

Because so much is involved with these two, I've broken them up into separate chapters. (We'll cover secondary shot headings in Chapter 2.)

Master Shot Headings do just what you'd think: They establish the master location for the scene.

This includes the 3-step formula most screenwriting practitioners are familiar with:

- Camera placement

- Location

- Time of day

You're no doubt familiar with examples such as:

```
INT. KREMLIN - DAY
EXT. CENTRAL PARK - NIGHT
INT./EXT. JIMMY'S '57 CHEVY -
NIGHT
```

Master shot headings can also get as complicated as:

```
EXT. SATURN - SPACE STATION -
ALPHA WING - LANDING PLATFORM
```

Here are the basics of creating master shot headings:

Tip No.1: Embrace your inner capitalization. Shot headings, both master and secondary, are always in CAPS. ALWAYS.

Tip No.2: Inside or Out. All master shot headings must begin with the abbreviation INT. or EXT. (interior and exterior respectively). Even if it's in space. Or the belly of a whale. Or inside Lindsay Lohan's brain.

Tip No.3: Move in, don't move out. Master shot headings always go from the general to the more specific.

It's…

```
INT. MANHATTAN - OFFICE
BUILDING - JIM'S OFFICE
```

NOT...

```
INT. JIM'S OFFICE - OFFICE
BUILDING - BROOKLYN
```

Tip No. 4: Keep your headings fixed to a single place. Master shot headings refer to a specific place. (EASTER is not a place, nor is DARKNESS, nor is the EDGE OF MADNESS — all of which I've seen in spec scripts.)

"Ask Yourself One Question: Do I Feel Lucky?"

Confused yet? Good! That means you're learning.

Now, let's tackle some of the most frequently asked questions screenwriters have about master shot headings to clear up any confusion before we move forward.

How do you know if it's an exterior or an interior?

I could be a smart-ass and say interior is indoors and exterior is outdoors.

But things like cars and outdoor stadiums can be perplexing. (Cars are INT. locations, even convertibles. Stadiums are EXT. Locations.)

The thing to ask is: Where am I putting the camera? Is this "on location?" Or could this theoretically be shot on a set?

General rule: If it's outdoors, and is not a man-made structure, it's probably an EXT. If it's inside, it's most likely an INT. (Remember: Exteriors are way more expensive to shoot. So keep them to a minimum in your script.)

What if I've got a scene where it goes back and forth between inside and outside?

If a pair of bloodthirsty ninjas are battling it out on the hood of a slow-moving golf cart, that can be written as:

INT./EXT. LOU'S GOLF CART - DAY

What if I've got lots of sub-locations in my master location?

It's easy. Just follow the rule that shot headings always go from the general to the specific.

This is why...

INT. PENNSYLVANIA - BATTLEFIELD - GENERAL GRANT'S TENT - DAY

... is accurate. But...

INT. KITCHEN - PAM'S HOUSE - THE BRONX - NIGHT

...is not.

What if I have a scene at sunset? How do I write that?

Time of day isn't just DAY or NIGHT.

Time of Day can also be LATE AFTERNOON or SUNSET or 9:32 A.M. or TEN MINUTES LATER or 1066 A.D.

Just make sure there's a compelling reason for

that kind of specificity in your master shot heading. (And not just because your OCD is kicking in.)

The logistics of getting a film crew to shoot at "sunset" is a headache most productions, especially those working on a newbie script, won't want to deal with.

What if I have different rooms in the same location? Do I need a master heading for each room?

Now we're getting somewhere. What you're really asking is: How do I write this without annoying the reader? (A step in the right direction.)

Here's the key: If the characters move from one place to another, but all within the same location, then you would write one master shot heading. (And then write a secondary heading for each new sub-location.)

So this would work:

```
INT. CHIP'S MANSION - MASTER
BEDROOM - NIGHT

Chip holds a glass of red wine up
```

to the light. Staring. Looking for
answers.

CHIP
But that would mean I was poisoned
by someone who lives in this
house.

KITCHEN

The Mansion Cook stirs a saucepot.
She reaches into her pocket and
pulls out a small glass vial and
pours its contents into the soup.

Something like this would be total overkill:

INT. CHIP'S MANSION - MASTER
BEDROOM - NIGHT

Chip holds a glass of Mountain Dew
up to the light.

CHIP
But that would mean I was poisoned

by someone who lives...here.

INT. CHIP'S MANSION - KITCHEN -
NIGHT

The House Cook stirs a saucepot.
She reaches into her pocket and
pulls out a small glass vial and
pours its contents into the soup.

We'll get to secondary shot headings in the next
chapter, but for now just remember most readers
SKIP over master shot headings.

So don't depend on them to do all the heavy
lifting. Keep your master headings simple, and focus
on the scene description and dialogue to tell most of
the story. (Most of the time, it's the only thing
development people look at anyway.)

Chapter 1 Key Takeaways:

- **Shot headings (also known as sluglines or scene headings) are an important part of screenplay format.** Mostly because they tell the reader WHERE they are.

- **Shot headings should be written in ALL CAPS.** Always. No exceptions.

- **The first element of a shot heading always begin with INT.** (denoting interior) or EXT. (denoting exterior). If it's outdoors and on location, it's probably an EXT. (Note: Cars, even convertibles, are INT.'s.)

- **The second element of a shot heading is location.** This can be as simple as INT. PARIS or as complicated as INT. PARIS - MOULIN ROUGE - CLAIRE'S DRESSING ROOM.

- **The location part of a shot heading always goes from general to specific.** Think about it from a camera perspective — wide shot, then move in closer.

- **Good shot headings are fixed to a single location.** No abstract bull crap needed.

- **Bouncing back and forth between inside and outside for a specific scene**, such as a fight sequence, can be written as INT./EXT. Just remember to keep it simple and clear.

- **If your scene involves numerous sub-locations**, within a central location, then use subheadings to avoid confusion and clutter. (Which we'll cover in the next chapter.)

Chapter 2:
Secondary Shot Headings (for Fun and Profit)

"A writer is someone for whom writing is more difficult than it is for other people."

-Thomas Mann

Quick confession: I hate camera shit in screenplays.

I hate anything that screams "Look at Me! I'm making the camera move."

That being said, there's an elegant and correct way to use secondary scene headings to show camera moves in a scene.

And let's be clear, that's what secondary scene

headings mean to a film crew: "Oh, crap, the writer is making us pick up this ultra-heavy Fuji GX680 and move it ten feet."

"It's the Pictures That Got Small"

Before I show you how to use secondary shot headings correctly, let's go over some ground rules.

Secondary shot headings:

- Are part of the master location.

- Show a focus or move for the camera.

- Contain NO ACTION, just WHO/WHAT/HOW we're looking at something.

- Where most writers throw in crap they don't need.

Lost? Don't worry. It's easy.

Here are the TOP six ways to use a secondary shot heading in your script:

- Insert Shots (E.g.: Letters or invitations — stuff you gotta read)

- Close-Ups

- Angles

- POV (Point of View)

- Subject Change

- Moving Shots

- Reverse Angles

Let's dig in!

No.1: Insert Shots

When the viewer needs to read something, like reading the text on a handwritten note, use INSERT, not CLOSE ON. (And be sure to capitalize whatever text is to be read.)

Something like:

INSERT - LETTER

Handwritten: DEAR JOHN, OUR LOVE MUST END. PAM.

Not...

CLOSE UP ON A LETTER

"Dear John, Our love must end! - Pam"

No.2: CLOSE UPS

If I read one more "WE CLOSE IN ON..." in a spec script, I swear I'm going to lose it.

First off, who the hell is this "we" you're talking about? (The director? The star? The writer's mother?)

And secondly, there's a much better way to do this. Here's some more elegant ways to pull this off:

```
CLOSE - QUEEN'S FACE
CLOSE ON QUEEN'S FACE
CLOSE ANGLE ON QUEEN'S FACE
```

Truth be told, I prefer the first one; seems to stand out on the page more. You can also do a variety of shots* this same way.

```
WIDE SHOT - DISNEYLAND
MED. SHOT - DISNEYLAND (Don't
spell out medium)
AERIAL SHOT - DISNEYLAND
TWO SHOT - MICKEY AND MINNIE
THREE SHOT - MICKEY, MINNIE AND
GOOFY
```

*But tread carefully with formatting strategies such as these. Like a Will Ferrell movie, they can get out-of-hand rather quickly.

No.3: Angles

Another cool way to indicate a camera move is to introduce a new, different angle into your scene. (Less intrusive than something like a WIDE SHOT and shows you're thinking visually.)

Suppose Batman is drinking a latte at a Gotham City Barnes and Noble. But we want to get a view of him from the ceiling where Spider-Man watches him intently.

We could do one of these:

```
DOWN ANGLE - BATMAN
ANGLE ON BATMAN
ANGLE - BATMAN
NEW ANGLE - BATMAN
```

Just be sure not to include any action in your scene heading. If you NEED to describe action in your angle description, do something like:

```
ANGLE ON BATMAN
drinking his latte, a foam
mustache forms on his face.
```

No.4: POV

If we wanted a more subjective view of Batman, say from Spider-Man's perspective, we'd write it like this:

```
SPIDER-MAN'S POV - BATMAN
```

or...

```
SPIDER-MAN'S POV
Batman sipping on a peppermint
latte.
```

To get back to the original POV, just throw in a good old:

BACK TO SCENE

No.5: Subject Change

In this secondary heading, the subject of the shot changes, but the scene is still within the existing location.

This "subject" can be virtually anything. A Rhino. Mt. Everest. My Uncle Lou who eats four Pop Tarts a day. Here's an example:

```
INT. WHITE HOUSE - PRESS ROOM -
DAY

The WHITE HOUSE PRESS CORPS loads
water into state-of-the-art water
rifles.

THE PRESIDENT
aims a water bazooka at the Press
Corps.
```

Notice how the shift from the Press Corps to the President introduced the element of surprise as you read it. (Instead of giving away the joke by describing The President from the outset.)

The nice part about a subject change is it doesn't feel camera-y when done well. (And breaks up blocks of text nicely.)

No.6: Moving Shots

If you have a scene where we're following the fast-paced movement of characters, then instead of typing new master headings every paragraph let me introduce you to my two best friends:

`MOVING WITH` and `TRACKING`.

Suppose you've got Bert and Ernie from "Sesame Street" chasing each other on mopeds during the Rose Bowl Parade.

Instead of writing every single frickin' street they cross you could just do:

`Burt and Ernie sneer at each other. The chase is on.`

MOVING WITH ROSE BOWL PARADE

Or you could do....

Bert and Ernie sneer. The chase is on.

TRACKING - BERT and ERNIE

(Notice how they feel different, visually. But both are effective and don't add frilly camera crap.)

No.6: Reverse Angles

This is like our earlier POV shot heading, except in this case we aren't looking for a subjective shot. We just need a camera view from the opposite angle.

BILLY THE KID
brushes his coat back. Revealing his pistol in its holster.

REVERSE ANGLE

```
Jesse James reaches for his
pistol. BANG.  Too late. He drops
to the ground.
```

Okay, I know that was a lot of info. But don't you feel incredibly smart and ready to crush the screenwriting world?

Good.

Because now we're moving on to the truly FUN part of screenplays: narrative description.

Chapter 2 Key Takeaways:

- Sub headings indicate a change or move of the camera and do NOT involve action.

- **Insert shots are used when you want something "read" by the audience.** Just throw in a good old INSERT - LETTER and you'll be on your way.

- **Close-ups are best written either with CLOSE - LADY GAGA or CLOSE ON LADY GAGA.** Whatever you do, don't use CLOSE UP ON LADY GAGA or WE MOVE IN ON LADY GAGA.

- **Subheadings that describe the angle of the camera can be effective if done subtly.** ANGLE ON DONALD TRUMP is probably my favorite way to write angles. Though you can also do

ANGLE - DONALD TRUMP.

- Showing the POV (point-of-view) of a specific character is easy with subheadings. Just do MADONNA'S POV - WARREN BEATTY. Be sure there's a purpose to your POV shot, otherwise it'll appear artsy-fartsy.

- If you want to write a scene where the subject of the shot changes, but that subject has no dialogue and isn't part of the master shot, then you can throw in the character's name and make it a subheading. Don't put action on the same line as the subheading.

- If you intend the camera to follow action that moves through various locations you can use MOVING WITH or TRACKING. Make it clear what they're moving with or tracking with, or else it'll confuse the reader.

- Reverse angles are awesome. A REVERSE ANGLE shows the action 180 degrees from the master shot. Be sure, you have a purpose for the reverse angle; this dramatic device can be easily over-used.

Chapter 3:
It's About the Visuals, Stupid

"When in doubt, have a man come through the room with a gun in his hand."

-Raymond Chandler

And nowhere is that more evident than in the narrative description of a screenplay.

It's also where the best writing in the world happens.

Sure...you could grab a selection from the Oprah Book Club to get a two-page flowery description of a stream.

But with tight, rigid, economical, get-to-the-frickin-point writing — nothing beats screenwriting at its best.

Here's a bit from the awesome script (and underrated movie) "Brick" by Rian Johnson. (Years before he allegedly ruined the Star Wars franchise.)

With a sharp breath the line clicks dead just as a black mustang roars by.

Brendan drops the receiver and spins out of the booth.

There, another pay phone up the hill--empty.

Brendan turns to the black mustang, far down the street. A man's hand drops a cigarette butt from the driver's side window.

The mustang turns the corner, gone.

Brendan walks after it, finds the cigarette butt on the street. Still smoking.

Tell me that ain't frickin' art! I'm convinced if good old Mr. Hemingway were alive today, he'd be churning out action movies at a Key West Starbucks.

So...how do you write great stuff like that?

First, let's walk before we run. (I'll give you some cool tips on writing tight prose like that. Promise.)

But, let me walk you through the top four freakouts screenwriters have about scene description and how you can avoid them:

Freakout No.1: How the #$#% Do I Introduce Characters?

Here's the rule: the first time you introduce a speaking character capitalize their name.

The door opens. JOHN SMYTHE, 40s, but dresses like he's in an emo band, stands in the doorway.

If we don't know their name, or learn it later - and they speak - we still need the CAPS.

```
The door opens. ANGRY NEIGHBOR,
40s, but dresses like he's in an
emo band, stands in the doorway.
```

If the character is labeled with a "stock" name at first (Policeman, Barista, Cheerleader), but we learn their real name quite soon after the first reference, we can wait to CAPITALIZE their name until we learn it.

```
A Barista tackles the Robber. This
is JOHN MYERS. And he's been
waiting his whole life for this
moment.
```

SUPER IMPORTANT NOTE: If the character doesn't talk. Don't CAPITALIZE his/her name at all.

Freakout No.2: How the #$#% Do I Do Sound Effects?

There are three basic guidelines for using sound effects in screenplays:

1) If the sound happens ONSCREEN, and requires a SOUND EFFECT, then CAPITALIZE both the sound and the object creating the sound.

Jim starts the car. AWFUL TWEEN MUSIC PLAYS on the CAR RADIO

The Punisher pulls the trigger. The SHOTGUN BLASTS a hole in the wall.

2) If the sound happens OFFSCREEN, CAPITALIZE it.

Betty looks inside the dark cabin. Behind the tool shed, TWIN GIRLS are LAUGHING.

Bobby opens the cash register. A PISTOL COCKS behind him.

3) If it's an organic on-screen sound that does not require an effect, DO NOT CAPITALIZE.

This includes people:

- Talking

- Laughing

- Knocking

- Yelling

- Cheering

- Playing horrible music with their guitar

Freakout No.3: How the #$#% Do I Show Text Messages and Emails?

If what's contained in a text message needs to be shown on screen, here are a couple of ways you can approach it:

```
Matt sits on the couch, watching
```

TV with his parents. Bored.

There's an ANNOYING CHIME from his
PHONE. He looks at the screen:

"TOM: Dude. Where you at?"

Matt looks at his Dad. Types into
the PHONE:

"MATT: There's been a
complication."

Another good way to go, if you don't need the
back-and-forth between two people, would be:

Matt sits on the couch, watching
TV with his parents. Bored.

There's an ANNOYING DEATH METAL
RINGTONE from his phone. He looks
at the Caller ID screen: "Shady
Tom."

Email is slightly different. Really depends on
how long the email is. If you just need a line or two.

Go with:

Constance scans the email on her daughter's laptop. She stops at the last line:

"...how do i tell my mom im pregnant..."

Constance slams the laptop case down.

But if you've got a lengthy email - Meg Ryan and Tom Hanks spent a whole movie flirting this way (yawn) - write it like this:

INT. LOS FELIZ STARBUCKS - DAY

Meg Ryan on her laptop. She looks around to make sure nobody's watching. She opens the email message:

"From: Tom Hanks"

"Subject: 'You've Got Mail'

```
Sequel?"

Meg smiles. This is it - her
comeback.

"...thinking of having Megan Fox
as the female lead. You wouldn't
mind, would you?..."

Meg throws the laptop. The DELL
COMPUTER CRASHES against the wall.
```

Freakout No.4: How the #$#% Do I Write Description That Doesn't Suck?

Forget all that "write only what you can see and hear" crap.

Truth is: You can do a lot more with description than that.

But just like asking a girl out in high school, it helps if you're cool about it. Writing something like:

```
He stands there. Speechless.
```

Thinking how crazy things have
gotten in his life to this point.

...is cliché. But a master like Shane Black would
write: (From "Kiss, Kiss, Bang, Bang"):

Harry stands, blank. Utterly
FROZEN. The poster boy for
cognitive dissonance. (yes, they
have that.)

There's a rhythm to good screenplay description.
It's tight, minimalist, and it's way, way shorter than
you think it should be. (Perfectly suited for ADD-
afflicted studio execs.)

The best way I know how to really get good at
this, aside from writing a ton of it, is read how the
masters do it.

Some of my favorites are: Shane Black (again):
("Kiss Kiss, Bang Bang")

Headlights. Car approaching.
FLASHING LIGHTS. Cops.

Oh shit, oh shit, oh shit. They
frantically drag the corpse toward
a chain-link FENCE. Huffing,
grunting…

Susannah Grant: ("Erin Brockovich")

But he kisses her anyway. And for
the first time in so long, she
feels like something other than a
failure.

He pulls her into him, and she
lets herself be pulled.

Todd Solondz ("Happiness")

Billy stands on the terrace and
looks down. He sees palm trees. He
sees the ocean.

He sees a beautiful woman
sunbathing by the pool. Talk of
turkey and weather filter out to

him.

Though I can't pin down EXACTLY the formula for kick-ass screenplay description - it's more art than science - I do have a few tips to keep you on track:

- Do not write in the past tense. Everything happens NOW in a screenplay.

- Kill the passive voice. It's not: "Jimmy is standing," it's: "Jimmy stands."

- Kill adverbs. They are not your friend. Stick to verbs and nouns.

- Trim it down until it's spare and then trim some more.

One more thing: Check out the novels of Elmore Leonard, E. Annie Proulx or any authors of hard-boiled detective genre. Their writing will train you for tight, lean description.

This excerpt from Proulx's "The Shipping News" could have easily come from a well-written screenplay:

A great damp loaf of a body. At
six he weighed eighty pounds. At
sixteen he was buried under a
casement of flesh.

Head shaped like a crenshaw, no
neck, reddish hair brushed back.
Features as bunched as kissed
fingertips. Eyes the color of
plastic. The monstrous chin, a
freakish shelf jutting from the
lower face.

Hmmm...monstrous chin? Freakish shelf jutting
from the lower face? Sounds like a couple of studio
heads I know.

Chapter 3 Key Takeaways:

- **The best — and most economical — writing in the world is kick-ass screenplay description.** No doubt in my mind about this, so don't even try convincing me otherwise.

- **Introducing characters in a screenplay is easy.** If they speak, their name must be in ALL CAPS. If they don't, keep their name in lower caps. (Even if we don't know their name in the beginning, if they speak at all their name must be in ALL CAPS.)

- **Writing sound effects intimidates many new screenwriters but it's NO big deal.** If the sound happens on screen, then the SOUND and the OBJECT that creates it needs to be in ALL CAPS. If the sound happens off-screen then the SOUND should be in ALL CAPS. If it's an organic sound on screen, like laughing or crying or knocking, then no need to capitalize.

- **The cleanest way to write a text message in a screenplay is to write the name and message within quotes.** So it'd be: "JOE: I'll buy that for a dollar."

- **As for email, simply show the character is reading and put the text in quote.** She opens her Gmail. "FROM: Bob...i love you."

- **Good screenplay description is** a) full of verbs b) written in the present tense c) written in the active voice and d) as spare and lean as can be.

Chapter 4:
You Talkin' To Me? (Dialogue Formatting Tricks)

"What I like in a good author isn't what he says, but what he whispers."

-Logan Smith

Ah yes, dialogue. Everyone's favorite.

Dialogue has three parts to it:

- The words people say

- The people who say those words

- (Parentheticals) that directly relate to how the dialogue is expressed or the action that surrounds the dialogue

Most people know how dialogue, character names, and parentheticals look on the page, but here's a refresher, just in case you were raised in a kelp bed by jellyfish:

```
SANTA CLAUS
Come on, Rudolph! Don't hold out
on me. Where's the safe house?
(smashes the Xmas lights with his
fist)
I WANT MY MONEY!
```

Writing dialogue the right way is fairly easy. But there are a few situations that can be confusing.

Dialogue Situation No.1: Voice-Overs

Though Harrison Ford hated them in "Blade Runner," voice overs (V.O.), which describe speech from a character who is not visible, can be a very effective writing tool.

As long as you use them well.

Hint: Make sure the voice-over text does NOT directly describe the visual action that's taking place. (Having a character narrate the fact he's eating breakfast, while we watch him eating breakfast, is pure torture.)

Here's how you write it:

EXT. HOLLYWOOD BOULEVARD - NIGHT.

Paris Hilton walks down Hollywood Boulevard. Alone. Way past closing time.

PARIS HILTON
(V.O.)
Fame isn't everything, you know.

A PAPARAZZI runs up and snaps her picture. Shocked at first, she then poses.

```
PARIS HILTON
(V.O.)
Who am I kidding? It's wonderful.
```

If a character is speaking, and they are out of view of the camera, but in the same location, then you would use the (O.S.) OFF-SCREEN direction:

```
Batman checks his reflection in
the shop window.
```

```
PENGUIN
(O.S.)
Losing your edge, Batman.
```

```
Batman pivots to see the Penguin
point a laser gun at him.
```

Dialogue Situation No.2: Group Talk

So what do you do if you need a whole group of people to speak at the same time? Simple, just refer to them as a group.

Coach McKenzie stares at his
football team.

COACH MCKENZIE
"I came to kick some ass and chew
some bubblegum..."

The FOOTBALL TEAM smiles. Then
answers in unison.

FOOTBALL TEAM
"And I'm all out of bubblegum!"

(Note: The dialogue above is in quotations
because it is a quote from the very awesome movie
"Them" by John Carpenter.)

Dialogue Situation No.3: Songs

Songs are easy. Trust me.

All you've gotta do is type them in lower and
upper-case letters, with line breaks organized
according to the rhyme.

The President looks at the camera.

PRESIDENT
Nation. As a brave poet once
said...

He looks at his notes. Goes for
it. Looks back at the camera.

PRESIDENT
(solemnly)
"If you want to be my lover,
You gotta get with my friends..."

Dialogue Situation No.4: Accents

Be very careful with these. I know you want to
add authentic "flavor" to your script, but one writer's
affectation is another reader's personal outrage.

Still sometimes they are unavoidable:

GRETA GARBO
I vant to be alone.

```
SWAMP TRUCKER
Well, Greta, I reckon there ain't
no reason fur us both be alone.
```

And, yes, you can use them. But it's my strong recommendation you keep them to an absolute minimum.

Dialogue Situation No.5: Underlining Dialogue

Sometimes you just have to emphasize a certain piece of dialogue. Underlines work really well for this!

```
DOC HOLLIDAY
Just so you know...I will kill you
someday.
```

Whatever you do, don't use bold or italics to emphasize pieces of dialogue. Like most traditions of screenplay format, if you can't replicate it on a typewriter, then you shouldn't use it.

Dialogue Situation No.6: Parentheticals

I saved the best for last. Parentheticals are one of the most commonly used (and abused) forms of screenplay format. Mostly because nobody knows what the hell to do with them.

Parentheticals are used to either describe how a line should be performed, or what action is taking place during the dialogue.

The Four Big Rules of Parentheticals are:

- Don't capitalize the first word.

- Don't place a parenthetical at the end of a block of dialogue.

- Don't allow the parenthetical to run over four lines.

- And…you need not use the pronoun "he" or "she" as it is obvious from the character name.

An example of good parenthetical use would be:

```
Lady Gaga hands the former
Chairman of the Federal Reserve a
cup of coffee.

LADY GAGA
  (wryly)
Good mornin', sunshine.

ALAN GREENSPAN
  (holding his head)
How much DID I drink last night?
```

You've now got a Master's degree in the "Fab Four" of screenplay format: master shot heading, secondary shot heading, dialogue and scene descriptions.

If you do nothing else, nailing these four horsemen of format will help you handle 90% of all the script format issues you might encounter.

And then you'll be ready for the stuff that

writers love, and readers fear, camera-moving stuff. (Which we'll tackle in the next chapter.)

Chapter 4 Key Takeaways:

- **Voice overs are easy — you need a (V.O.) descriptor below the name of the character.** Make sure your character's (V.O.) adds something to the action. (And doesn't just echo what we can already see.)

- **When you want to have a GROUP OF PEOPLE say something in unison,** identify the group then write their dialogue as you would any single character.

- **Songs are written in lower-case, with appropriate line breaks.** You don't have to identify the song title, unless it is absolutely crucial.

- **Tread carefully with accents.** Things can go horribly wrong if you're not careful.

- **Underlining dialogue can be a great way to emphasize an important line.** Just remember, it's a nuclear option. You can use it a few times before it loses its potency.

- **Parentheticals describe the tone or emotion of how a given line should be delivered.** If you MUST use them be sure they a) are not capitalized b) do not run over four lines c) don't use pronouns to identify the speaker. (As this should be obvious.)

Chapter 5:
Transition This!

"If you can't explain it to a six-year-old, you don't understand it yourself."

-Albert Einstein

Transitions are used when a simple "cut" between scenes isn't sufficient. And they have their place.

But they're also some of the biggest film-school crap writers put into scripts.

Transitions include:

- Fades

- Cuts

- Dissolves

- Wipes

When done well, they can be effective for establishing pace. When done badly....

Peter Jackson used nearly five "FADE TO BLACK" transitions at the end of "The Return of the King" and, I would contend, with disappointing results.

So let's look at the different ways to use transitions in a subtle and non-obnoxious way:

Transition No.1: Fades

The two transitions nearly everyone knows are:

FADE IN:

THE KREMLIN

    and

FADE TO BLACK.

    Most scripts start with FADE IN and end with FADE TO BLACK, but this is not a hard and fast rule. If you begin your film with a smash cut, you know where the iris of the camera doesn't actually fade in, you might instead start your screenplay with something like:

THE KREMLIN

Darkness

    Or if you want to start with your first master shot heading that's okay too. (I've seen this rule broken enough times to know it's not really a rule.)

Transition No.2: CUT TOs

I'll be honest, and it's just an opinion, I really hate these. This is what they look like:

```
Bobby wipes down his 1978
Oldsmobile.

CUT TO:

EXT. GRAND PRIX RACE - DAY

Bobby makes the first turn in his
F-1 Stock Race Car.
```

First off, every scene is a cut. So why do you need a CUT TO to reinforce the point?

Some writers claim they need it for pace. I think it looks ancient. (Like something out of a William Goldman fever dream.)

Do you want to look old-fashioned? Do you want to look like you learned screenplay format out of the discontinued bin of your local library?

Don't use them. (Unless you sell your script, then you can do whatever the hell you want.)

Transition No.3: DISSOLVES

Dissolves aren't my favorite, but they're more of a misdemeanor than a felony. They imply the passage of time, something you can't quite get from a simple cut.

Jim gets down on one knee. Pulls out a ring. Jenny emphatically NODS.

DISSOLVE TO:

INT. HOSPITAL – MATERNITY WARD – DAY

Jenny, prepped for labor. Jim, filming the whole thing with a $3000 camcorder.

You can also do:

RIPPLE DISSOLVE TO:

This is the Scooby Doo flashback in effect. I'm not sure I'd want to use something from a stoner-cartoon in the 70s. But if you want to, knock yourself out.

Transition No.4: Wipes

I like these because they show forethought about the visual tableau of your story without appearing obnoxious.

You just gotta make sure you don't overdo it.

Wipes are where the first image of a new scene literally "wipes" over the last image of the previous scene.

```
NEWSPAPER BOY
throws a newspaper toward the
house. It SPINS -

WIPE TO:

INT. DAILY MAIL'S PRINTING PRESS

NEWSPAPERS SPIN by on a conveyor
belt.
```

Just remember that with transitions: you want to get in and get out. Don't spend a lot of time with them.

But add them if you feel your pacing isn't being conveyed with the script as is. Just leave the directing to the, you know, director.

Chapter 5 Key Takeaways:

- **Transitions in a screenplay can be necessary**, but they can also be pretentious. Like paprika, a little goes a long way.

- **Fades are probably the one transition everybody has heard of.** Most scripts start with a FADE IN and end with a FADE OUT. But this isn't set in stone. Start your story with a smash cut if you want.

- **Don't use FADE OUTs in the middle of your story** unless there's a real reason for it. Or you're Peter Jackson and you own half of New Zealand.

- **CUT-TOs are an old-fashioned way to show a sharp transition between scenes.** Some writers use them, but I'm not a fan.

- **DISSOLVES are a decent way to show time has passed.** Just be sure you want an effect that screams TV-movie.

- **WIPES are a cool way to transition from one scene to another.** Especially if the two scenes have a thematic connection. "Citizen Kane" did this, amongst other things, well.

Chapter 6:
Phone Calls, Montages and Flashbacks (Oh My!)

"Screenwriting is no more complicated than old French torture chambers."

-James L. Brooks

Okay, this chapter is going to be a kind of a free-for-all.

I was gonna call it "All the Crazy Shit You Wanna Do In Your Scripts, But Probably Shouldn't"...but I didn't want this book to go over 200 pages.

So here are the quirky weird things you've always

wanted to do with your screenplay format, but were afraid to ask.

No.1: Flashbacks/Dream Sequences

The tried-and-true approach to these is to have the word underlined at the beginning of a master shot heading.

So it would be:

FLASHBACK - INT. NORWEGIAN HOTEL - DAY

Or...

DREAM SEQUENCE - EXT. MONA'S BEDROOM - NIGHT

But one approach I've seen lately, and seems cleaner, is to go with:

INT. MONA'S BEDROOM - NIGHT [FLASHBACK]

Again, I like this approach because it doesn't feel intrusive. But both are acceptable.

And how do we end a flashback? Throw in an "end" heading at the far right of the page.

```
INT. WESTMINSTER ABBEY - DAY
[DREAM SEQUENCE]

Caroline slow-dances with a six-
foot tomato, as her third-grade
class looks on.

END DREAM SEQUENCE.
```

No.2: Phone Calls

I probably get more questions about how to format a phone call than any other screenwriting question.

That should tell you something. (That phone calls are inherently undramatic and most writers love them.)

But, in certain instances, a phone call can be a powerful tool. (Just don't let them drag. Yes, I'm talking to you "Twilight"!)

The key is to use the INTERCUT technique to establish you're bouncing between two different locations.

So here's how you write it:

```
INT. BATMAN'S LAIR - NIGHT

Batman picks up his cell phone.
Dials.

BATMAN
What'ya doin?

INT. SUPERMAN'S FORTRESS OF
SOLITUDE - NIGHT

Superman sits in a recliner in the
stark atmosphere of his ancestral
home.
```

```
SUPERMAN
Nothing. I'm so bored.

INTERCUT phone conversation.

BATMAN
I know, right? Ever since we
vanquished all evil from Earth....

SUPERMAN
(ruefully)
Things just aren't the same.
```

No.3: Montages

Whatever you do, don't read this part. Just skip to the end and please don't learn how to write a montage.

They're the worst thing to come to screenwriting since "cell phones not getting reception in the woods."

What...you're still here? All right, don't say I didn't warn you....

"Snakes. Why'd It Have to Be Snakes?"

I've seen montages written in many different ways. But I'll give you two that don't make me want to kill myself. (And that's high praise, believe me.)

Let's say we're writing a scene where Bill and Hilary Clinton are enjoying a romantic weekend in D.C. (Not likely, but let's pretend.)

We could do this:

```
AROUND WASHINGTON, D.C. - MONTAGE

A) EXT. WASHINGTON MONUMENT - DAY

Bill and Hilary have a picnic at
the base of the monument.

B) INT. SMITHSONIAN - DAY

Hilary looks for Bill. Can't find
him. Suddenly she sees him wave to
her from inside the Apollo 13
spacecraft.

C) INT. ITALIAN RESTAURANT - NIGHT
```

Bill and Hilary eat pasta, re-enacting the scene from "The Lady and the Tramp."

Or suppose we've got Superman and Lois Lane checking out the sights of good old NYC.

AROUND NEW YORK CITY - MONTAGE

Superman and Lois Lane stand in line for a pair of hoagies at Carnegie's Deli.

Superman and Lois Lane walk past a newsstand. Lois argues with a man selling her newspaper. Superman smiles awkwardly.

Superman and Lois sip champagne on top of the Empire State Building. They kiss. Suddenly, Lex Luthor vacuums them up into his large VACUUMATOR.

You're allowed to write montages. But my biased

preference is you do nothing that makes you look like you just graduated from a Learning Annex screenwriting class.

Even if you did.

Chapter 6 Key Takeaways:

- **There are a couple of different ways to write FLASHBACKS and DREAM SEQUENCES.** My favorite is just to add [FLASHBACK] or [DREAM SEQUENCE] at the end of a master shot heading. (To end the sequence just throw in an [END FLASHBACK] or [END DREAM SEQUENCE].)

- **Phone calls are easy as long as you use the INTERCUT direction.** Establish the two master locations for the conversation and then throw in a good old INTERCUT phone conversation into your script.

- **Montages are the bane of my existence.** They should not exist, and you should never write them.

- **But if write them try to keep them simple.** Start with an AROUND METROPOLIS - MONTAGE…and then break your parts of the montage into paragraphs.

Epilogue:
"Gonna Miss You Most of All Scarecrow"

Congratulations. You now know more about screenplay format than 99 percent of the screenwriters in the world.

Hell, you know more about format than most professional screenwriters working in the biz. (No joke.)

And if you're still not quite sure how to write your master shot headings or describe an ANGLE ON, don't worry.

You can still get these two FREE resources to help you out:

- A FREE PDF version of this book. (Just

drop me a line at
Michael@scriptbully.com with the
subject line "Gimme My Format PDF"
and I'll send it right over.)

- A sample screenwriting scene that uses all
  the techniques outlined in this book,
  including voice-overs, close-ups,
  montages, camera effects, etc. which can
  be found at my blog:
  http://scriptbully.com/screenplay-
  format-sample

Print it out. Frame it. Tattoo it on your back.
Whatever. I don't care.

Just don't let the techniques of screenplay
format stop you from writing your pages.

A well-meaning writer could spend months, if
not years, trying to master screenplay format.

Don't.

Just keep churning out those scripts, and your
mastery of format will come.

And if you keep writing and writing - I find screenwriters really crush it on their third or fourth script - a magical thing happens: Craft meets inspiration.

You produce some of the most amazing work of your life. And then you can write as many montages as your heart desires.

Talk soon…and if you'd like to drop me a line, just email me over at michael@scriptbully.com. Thanks!

Appendix: Scripts I Mentioned

Chapter Five:

- "Butch Cassidy and the Sundance Kid" by William Goldman (Great for dialogue, and for realizing how old-school the formatting used to be)
- "Brick"by Rian Johnson (Taut, tight film-noir type writing)
- "Kiss Kiss, Bang Bang" by Shane Black (Great for learning how to write stylized, great description)
- "Erin Brockovich" by Sussannah Grant (Great for writing character directions, that don't read like character directions)
- "Hapiness" by Todd Solondz (Zen-like minimalism and irony)
- "The Shipping News" by E. Annie Prolux (A novel as spare as any screenplay you'll ever find
- "Them" by John Carpenter (Managing a big cast)

Also By Michael Rogan

Grab the ENTIRE ScriptBully screenwriting collection today! It's like FIVE screenwriting books in ONE.

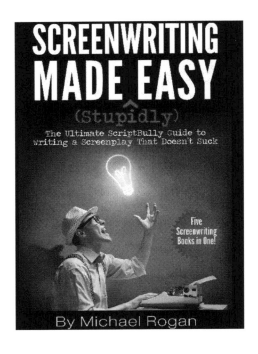

Don't Forget:
A Special FREE Gift for You!

If you'd like FREE instant access to my seminar "7 Secrets to a Kick-Ass and Marketable Screenplay" then head over to **ScriptBully.com/Free**. (What else you gonna do? Watch another "Twilight" movie?!)

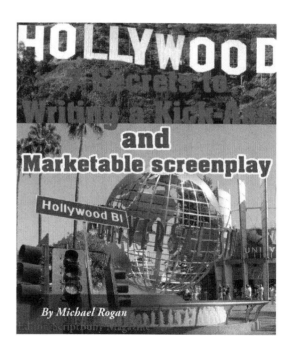

DISCLAIMER AND/OR LEGAL NOTICES: Every effort has been made to accurately represent this book and it's potential. Results vary with every individual, and your results may or may not be different from those depicted. No promises, guarantees or warranties, whether stated or implied, have been made that you will produce any specific result from this book. Your efforts are individual and unique, and may vary from those shown. Your success depends on your efforts, background and motivation.

The material in this publication is provided for educational and informational purposes only and is not intended as medical advice. The information contained in this book should not be used to diagnose or treat any illness, metabolic disorder, disease or health problem. Always consult your physician or health care provider before beginning any nutrition or exercise program. Use of the programs, advice, and information contained in this book is at the sole choice and risk of the reader.

Printed in Great Britain
by Amazon